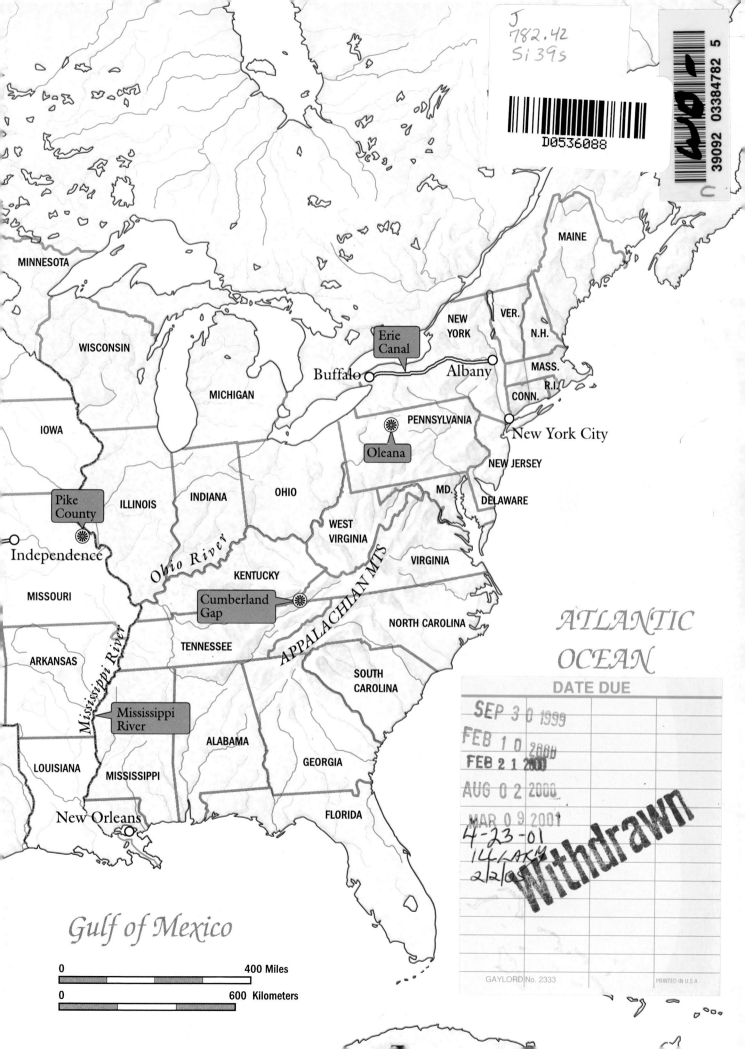

MINNESOTA

WISCONSIN

IOWA

MICHIGAN

MAINE

NEW
YORK

VER.

N.H.

Erie
Canal

MASS.

Buffalo

Albany

R.I.

CONN.

PENNSYLVANIA

New York City

Oleana

NEW JERSEY

Pike
County

ILLINOIS

INDIANA

OHIO

MD.

DELAWARE

Independence

Ohio River

WEST
VIRGINIA

VIRGINIA

MISSOURI

KENTUCKY

Cumberland
Gap

APPALACHIAN MTS.

NORTH CAROLINA

ARKANSAS

TENNESSEE

Mississippi River

ATLANTIC

OCEAN

SOUTH
CAROLINA

Mississippi
River

ALABAMA

GEORGIA

LOUISIANA

MISSISSIPPI

New Orleans

FLORIDA

Gulf of Mexico

0   400 Miles

0   600 Kilometers

SINGING OUR WAY WEST

SONGS AND STORIES OF AMERICA'S WESTWARD EXPANSION

JERRY SILVERMAN

THE MILLBROOK PRESS
BROOKFIELD, CONNECTICUT

Cover photograph courtesy of North Wind Picture Archives

Photographs courtesy of Museum of the City of New York: p. 7;
Culver Pictures: p. 11; The Granger Collection, New York: pp. 12, 18;
North Wind Picture Archives: pp. 24, 47, 60, 66; The Mariners'
Museum, Newport News, Virginia: p. 29; Friends of the Governor's
Mansion, Austin, Texas: p. 36; Corbis-Bettmann: p. 42 (top); Crocker
Art Museum, Sacramento, California: E. B. Crocker Collection: p. 42
(bottom); The Bancroft Library: p. 48; Library of Congress: pp. 54,
72 (#USZ62-737), 78; Pueblo Library District: p. 61.
Endpaper map by Joe LeMonnier.

The Library of Congress classifies this book as a musical score,
therefore Cataloging-in-Publication Data is not available.
ISBN 0-7613-0417-7

Published by The Millbrook Press, Inc.
2 Old New Milford Road
Brookfield, Connecticut 06804

 **Contents**

 Introduction

Come all you bold Britons, wherever you be,
I would have you draw near and listen to me.
The times they grow harder in England every day;
It is much better living in North Americay.[1]

This verse from the song "An Invitation to North America" expressed the feelings of a great many British families in the eighteenth century. The British colonies in eastern North America, with their fields ready to be farmed and their forests teeming with wild life, were an irresistible lure—and thousands answered the call. But with the Declaration of Independence in 1776, the American Revolution, and the establishment of the United States of America, a whole new element was added. Heretofore unimaginable words like "freedom," "democracy," and "elections" spread like wildfire throughout the old continent. These high-sounding ideas combined with the down-to-earth reality of virtually unlimited land in "North Americay," and the flow, the rush across the western ocean, was on!

By the end of nineteenth century, the wave of humanity fleeing the old ways and hoping for a fresh start in the New World had grown into the millions, as immigrants from all over Europe poured into America.

The Germans sang:

Today's the day and now's the hour,
We travel to America.
The wagon is prepared to start.
With wife and children we depart.[2]

The Swedes joined the chorus:

We must cross the salty waves,
Brothers, get in motion,
And we'll reach America,
Far across the ocean.[3]

The Italians chimed in:

Merica, Merica, Merica,
What will it be, this America.
Merica, Merica, Merica,
A beautiful garden of flowers.[4]

Jews, fleeing persecution, added joyously:

Columbus, I give you the first prize.
To you, my America, likewise.
All is fine as fine can be,
Jews, all sing along with me
Columbus, I give you the first prize;
And to you, America, likewise.[5]

These are but four examples of songs that reflect the attitudes of some of the masses of people that flocked to our shores in the nineteenth and early twentieth centuries. The flow of immigrants continues to this very day—but that's another story.

It was clear to one and all, practically from the beginning of the settlement of North America, that the eastern seaboard could not contain all the people that were continually arriving. The cry of "Go west, young man!," expressed by the nineteenth-century newspaper editor Horace Greeley, echoed throughout the new nation. And go west they did. "Young men," blazing the trail, were soon to be followed by others—young and old, men and women, entire families.

*Tens of thousands of European immigrants arrived in America
during the nineteenth and early twentieth centuries—some never
knowing that the grueling ocean passage was merely the first step
in their journey westward in search of a new life.*

By 1845 a new concept had entered the national consciousness: Manifest Destiny. It put forth the idea that Americans are a chosen people, blessed with free institutions and ordained by God to create a model society in the wilderness. In practical terms it translated into the desire to extend the boundaries of the United States to the Pacific

Ocean no matter who or what stood in the way, including the Spanish in Florida, the Mexicans from Texas to California, the French in Louisiana, the British in Washington and Oregon, the Russians in Alaska, and the Native Americans who populated the entire continent.

Other people whose interests were certainly not taken into consideration in the opening up of the land were the Negro slaves. They, like the Native Americans, were merely considered as part of the landscape. The overriding issue that confronted the American people before the Civil War, as the frontier moved westward, was how to determine which new states should be "slave" and which should be "free." When the Civil War and the Emancipation Proclamation of 1863 settled that question once and for all, the newly freed black population still could not identify with the Fourth of July orators who thundered their espousal of Manifest Destiny.

As far as the Indians—the Native Americans—were concerned, their destiny was to be pushed off their ancestral lands by treaty or force and relegated to desolate areas, called reservations.

❋

The question of who really discovered America—Leif Ericsson or Christopher Columbus—is sometimes answered by "neither." How can a land be "discovered" when it is already populated? The native people who lived there did not feel that they had been discovered; they knew where they were. The settling of the West can be looked at from the same point of view. The land was already occupied when first the Europeans and then the Americans moved in.

In any mass migration of people, such as took place in this country in the eighteenth and nineteenth centuries, there is bound to be some pushing and shoving. What would have happened if the Algonquins, Iroquois, Apaches, and Comanches had sailed eastward across the Atlantic in, say, 1491, and "discovered" England? Would they have been welcomed with open arms as bearers of a new and better civilization, or would there have been some pushing and shoving?

Well, that didn't happen. We can't rewrite history, we can only record and study it. What we are left with are the facts of the largest population shift in human history—and the thoughts, writings, and songs of those who made the journey.

Cumberland Gap

My home's across the Smoky Mountains,
My home's across the Smoky Mountains,
My home's across the Smoky Mountains,
And I'll never get to see you any more, more, more,
And I'll never get to see you any more.[7]

Whenever people have faced a mountain, they have always wondered what lay on the other side. Another old song tells us that "The bear went over the mountain to see what he could see/And what do you think he saw?/The other side of the mountain...."

The desire to see "the other side of the mountain" drove early American settlers ever westward from their original homes along the Atlantic seaboard. The first great range of mountains that got in their way were the Appalachians, which stretch from Newfoundland, Canada, in the north some 1,500 miles (2,400 kilometers) southwestward to central Alabama.

The only way the pioneers could cross the Appalachians was to locate "passes" between two mountain ridges that were wide and smooth enough for their wagons to make it across. But before any wagons could set out on what was at best an uncomfortable journey, advance trailblazers had to go by foot to see if such passes even existed. In the 1700s this kind of exploration was risky business. You never knew what dangers might be lurking along a trail that led to the other side of the mountain. Sudden storms, rock slides, wild animals, hostile Indians (not all Indians were hostile, but you never knew), and the ever-present possibility of just plain getting lost kept all but the bravest at home. As it turned out, however, there were always enough brave ones to lead the way.

In 1750 a party of Virginians led by Thomas Walker was exploring the region where the present-day states of Virginia, Kentucky, and Tennessee come together. They came upon a particularly beautiful stretch of country that included a range of mountains (part of the Appalachians), a river, and a gap (another name for a mountain pass). Since they were all loyal subjects of the king of England, they chose an English nobleman, the duke of Cumberland, in whose honor they named their discoveries. So it was that the mountains came to be called the Cumberland Mountains, the river the Cumberland River, and the gap the Cumberland Gap.

Seventeen years after the Walker expedition explored and named the Cumberland region, another pioneer entered the Gap "to see what he could see." The year was 1767. His name was Daniel Boone.

Daniel Boone was born in Pennsylvania in 1734. As a young man he moved with his family to the Yadkin Valley of North Carolina, about 40 miles (64 kilometers) east of the Blue Ridge range of the Appalachians. Young Daniel began hunting and trapping in the wilderness near his home. He soon developed a reputation as a skilled woodsman and explorer, and his wanderings eventually took him as far south as Florida and as far west as Missouri.

It was in 1767 that he first entered the Cumberland Gap with a group of hunters. He didn't completely traverse the Gap on this first visit, but in the years between 1769 and 1771 he and several companions trapped and hunted for furs and skins throughout its whole length and into Kentucky. The land was rich in wildlife, and the fertile soil on the Kentucky side of the Gap was soon to prove an irresistible lure for land-hungry settlers.

In 1775, Boone led a party of settlers through the Gap to the south bank of the Kentucky River, where they established the town of Boonesboro. He helped negotiate the purchase of the land from the Cherokees, hoping that this would ensure peace between the settlers and the Indians. But Cherokee chief Dragging Canoe was not happy with the terms of the treaty. He promised that the land would be "a dark and bloody one." Unfortunately, his prediction turned out to be all too true. From 1775 to 1782, Kentuckians and Indians fought each other as far north as Detroit, Michigan, and Kaskaskia, Illinois.

Nevertheless, during this period the Cumberland Gap acted as a magnet for increasing numbers of settlers. By the end of the Revolu-

The trail through the Cumberland Gap eventually became America's first national highway. Begun in 1811, the 500-mile (800-kilometer) road was used by the pioneers to travel to the West, as well as by the cattlemen to drive their livestock back to the East.

tionary War (1783) some 12,000 adventurous souls had crossed the Gap into the new territory. By 1792 the population was more than 100,000, and Kentucky was admitted to the Union.

The trail leading through the Gap was called the Wilderness Road. By 1800 more than 300,000 people had made the westward journey through the Gap. What was of equal importance to this westward movement was the reverse flow of livestock. At least as many head of cattle were driven east through the Gap each year.

Until the 1820s and 1830s, when the Erie, the Pennsylvania Main Line, and the Chesapeake and Ohio canals began to offer an easier, more attractive passage west, the Cumberland Gap was the most important gateway in the irreversible tide of western settlement. The

*Troops under the command of General Ambrose Burnside
occupied the Cumberland Gap during the American Civil War,
thus regaining control of the strategic passageway for the Union.*

crowded eastern states had literally pushed eager pioneers through the Gap and into the rich lands of "old Kaintuck." They said that the corn grew so fast out there that "a man had to step out of the way to keep from being carried over the tree tops." Boone himself, whose later explorations took him beyond the Mississippi, said, "I have never found but one Kentucky—a spot on earth where nature seems to have concentrated all her bounties."

The strategic value of the Cumberland Gap was recognized during the Civil War. Its location at the meeting point of Virginia, Tennessee, and Kentucky made it a prize worth fighting for, and some fierce battles did take place in the region, with control of the Gap swinging back and forth between Union and Confederate forces. The song refers to the victory of Confederate general Braxton Bragg's forces over those of Union general George Morgan in September 1862 in "the blue-grass land" (Kentucky). But in September 1863, Union troops under the command of General Ambrose E. Burnside finally secured the Cumberland Gap for the North, under whose control it remained for the rest of the war.

RECOMMENDED LISTENING

Each of the recordings listed here and in succeeding chapters under "Recommended Listening" contains the song discussed in that chapter, as well as a number of other interesting songs.

Ralph Stanley, *Ralph Stanley and the Clinch Mountain Boys.* Rebel 4001.

New Lost City Ramblers, *There Ain't No Way Out*, Smithsonian Collection Recordings, 40098

Doc Watson and Clarence Ashley, *Original Folkways Recordings*, Smithsonian Collection Recordings, 40029.

The Carter Family, *On Border Radio*, Vol. 1, Arhoolie 411.

CUMBERLAND GAP

2) The first white man in Cumberland Gap,
The first white man in Cumberland Gap,
The first white man in Cumberland Gap,
Was Doctor Walker, an English chap.

3) Daniel Boone on Pinnacle Rock, (x3)
He killed Indians with an old flintlock.

4) Cumberland Gap is a noted place, (x3)
Three kinds of water to wash your face.

5) Cumberland Gap with its cliff and rocks, (x3)
   Home of the panther, bear, and fox.

6) September mornin' in sixty-two, (x3)
   Morgan's Yankees all withdrew.

7) They spiked Long Tom* on the mountain top, (x3)
   And over the cliffs they let him drop.

8) They burned the hay, the meal, and the meat, (x3)
   And left the Rebels nothing to eat.

9) Braxton Bragg with his Rebel band, (x3)
   He run George Morgan to the blue-grass land.

10) Ef it's not here when I come back, (x3)
    I'll raise Hell in Cumberland Gap.

11) Ol' Aunt Dinah took a little spell, (x3)
    Broke my little jug all to Hell.

12) I've got a woman in Cumberland Gap, (x3)
    She's got a boy that calls me "pap."

13) Me and my wife and my wife's grand'pap, (x3)
    All raise Hell in Cumberland Gap.

* Long Tom (or Old Tom)—a heavy cannon located on top
  of Cumberland Mountain.

Fifteen Years on the Erie Canal

Oh, the E-ri-e was a-rising,
And the gin was a-getting low,
And I scarcely think we'll get a drink,
Till we get to Buffalo-o-o-
Till we get to Buffalo.[8]

There was another way that easterners could make their way through the mountainous wilderness that blocked their way to points west—by water, or more specifically, by canal. A canal is something like a river—but not quite. A river is a natural waterway. A canal, which links two other bodies of water (a lake to a river, for example), is constructed by people. It has to be dug out. When completed, the water pours in from either end and vessels can pass from one end to the other.

The Hudson River, which flows southward into the Atlantic Ocean, is a great natural break in the Appalachian chain of mountains. In the eighteenth and nineteenth centuries, ships were able to sail the river from New York City to Albany and back. New York was the most important port on the East Coast for goods and people coming from Europe. But, as we have seen, it was very difficult for those goods and people to break free of the eastern seaboard and move westward to the open land that awaited them.

Buffalo, on the shore of Lake Erie, lies some 300 miles (480 kilometers) west of Albany. Although the terrain is relatively level, no real roads connected those two cities. There were some trails through the forests, but nothing wide enough and smooth enough for any kind of reliable wagon traffic. Those wagons that did struggle through took more than two weeks to make the trip. If there were only some way to open up an easier passage between Albany and Buffalo, that would link New York City (and Europe) with the Great Lakes and the vast fertile plains and future cities that were bound to spring up.

De Witt Clinton (1769–1828) knew what had to be done. Clinton was mayor of New York City for various periods between 1803 and 1815. In 1810 he was a member of a commission set up to explore a route for a canal between Lake Erie and the Hudson River. In 1811 he went to Washington to seek federal aid for the project, but was unsuccessful. There was war brewing between the United States and Great Britain (the War of 1812), and there was no money available for such an expensive undertaking.

However, the idea of such a canal so captured the popular imagination, that in 1816 the commission was revived, this time with Clinton as president. Construction was begun in 1817, and a 15-mile (25-kilometer) section was opened between Utica and Rome in 1819. It was an immediate success. Clinton's popularity was so enhanced by his connection with the canal that he was elected governor of New York in 1817. He served two three-year terms until 1823 and was reelected in 1825. Work on the canal continued while he was in and out of office, and on October 25, 1825, it was officially opened in its entire length. Governor Clinton traveled triumphantly on the *Seneca Chief* from Buffalo to Albany with two kegs of Lake Erie water, which was symbolically poured into the Atlantic Ocean in New York Harbor.

Twenty years later, Michigan had increased its population sixty-fold and Ohio had climbed from the thirteenth to the third most heavily populated state in the Union. The Erie Canal, the longest canal in the world at that time, was the highway for most of these settlers and their goods. Clinton's 363-mile (585-kilometer) "ditch" had proven itself. The way was now open to the Midwest and beyond.

❈

The Erie Canal was built solely by humans and horses. Supplies had to be brought in little by little as the digging progressed, since there were no roads along the route. From the Albany-Troy region starting point, the way west followed the Mohawk Valley through virtual wilderness. It was called a water-level route because it did not cross high

Horses or mules, attached to long ropes, pulled the boats by walking along the towpath on the bank of the Erie Canal. Low bridges crossed over the canal at regular intervals, and the canal boat operators had to watch their heads as they passed under them.

elevations, although it did rise some 500 feet (152 meters) on its way to Lake Erie. The passage of the canal boats was accomplished by the use of eighty-two locks—watertight compartments that, when filled with water, lifted or lowered the boats to the next higher or lower level. The trip took a leisurely six days, although passenger packets drawn by relays of fresh horses could cover the distance in about half that time.

The success of the canal had a direct effect on the growth and development of the entire region through which it passed. New York City, Albany, and Buffalo grew rapidly in size and importance. Passengers and freight traffic flowed between New England and New York and the rapidly growing states of Ohio, Indiana, Illinois, and Michigan. Settlers and manufactured goods streamed westward in ever-increasing numbers. Ships on the Great Lakes bearing grain from the rich farmlands of the Midwest, as well as beef and pork from the stockyards, could now deliver their cargo directly to Buffalo, from where it would be shipped down to New York and even on to Europe. The growing foreign trade assured that New York would remain the most important port on the East Coast—ahead of Boston, Philadelphia, and Baltimore.

New York had become the true Empire State, and the Erie Canal, only 4 feet (122 centimeters) deep, had become the superhighway on the way to the West!

RECOMMENDED LISTENING

Pete Seeger, *Children's Concert at Town Hall*. Legacy Records 46185.

Bob Gibson, *Joy, Joy!* Riverside Records 9909.

The Weavers, *The Weavers' Greatest Hits*. Vanguard 15/16.

FIFTEEN YEARS ON THE ERIE CANAL

By Thomas S. Allen

I've got a mule and her name is Sal, Fif - teen years on the
good old work - er and a good old pal, Fif - teen years on the

E - rie Ca - nal. She's a
E - rie Ca - nal. We've hauled some barg - es in our day,

Filled with lum - ber, coal and hay, and we know ev - 'ry inch of the way, From

Chorus

Al - ba - ny to Buf fa - lo. Low bridge, ev - 'ry - bo - dy down, Low bridge, For we're

Lyrics under the music:
com- ing to a town. And you'll al- ways know your neigh- bor, You'll al- ways know your pal, If you've
ev - er nav - i - gat - ed on the E - rie Ca - nal. We E - rie Ca - nal.

2) We better be on our way old pal,
   Fifteen years on the Erie Canal.
   'Cause you bet your life I'd never part from Sal,
   Fifteen miles on the Erie Canal.
   Get up there, mule, here come a lock,
   We'll make Rome 'bout six o'clock.
   One more trip and back we'll go,
   Right back home to Buffalo. *Chorus*

3) Oh, where would I be if I lost my pal?
   Fifteen years on the Erie Canal.
   Oh, I'd like to see a mule as good as Sal,
   Fifteen years on the Erie Canal.
   A friend of mine once got her sore,
   Now, he's got a broken jaw.
   'Cause she let fly with her iron toe
   And kicked him into Buffalo. *Chorus*

4) I don't have to call when I want my Sal,
   Fifteen years on the Erie Canal;
   She trots from her stall like a good old gal,
   Fifteen years on the Erie Canal,
   I eat my meals with Sal each day
   I eat beef and she eats hay,
   She ain't so slow if you want to know,
   She put the "Buff" in Buffalo. *Chorus*

5) You'll soon hear them sing all about my gal,
   Fifteen years on the Erie Canal,
   It's a darned fool ditty 'bout my darned fool Sal,
   Fifteen years on the Erie Canal.
   Oh, every band will play it soon,
   Darned fool words and darned fool tune;
   You'll hear it sung everywhere you go,
   From Mexico to Buffalo. *Chorus*

 Oleana

Well, I came to America because I heard the streets were paved with gold. When I got here I found out three things: first, the streets weren't paved with gold; second, they weren't paved at all; and third, I was expected to pave them.

> — Recollections of an Italian immigrant,
> Ellis Island Museum

In 1853 a Norwegian songwriter named Ditmar Meidel composed a funny song about a place in Pennsylvania called Oleana. Although he had never set foot in America, Meidel was able to write verse after verse about life in Oleana to the catchy tune that he had composed. His clever and humorous descriptions of daily life in Oleana caught the imagination of his compatriots, and his song, "Oleana," was soon being sung all across Norway and in Norwegian settlements in America.

There was only one problem with the words of the song: They were completely untrue.

Ole Bull (1810–1880) was a famous Norwegian violinist. He studied the violin in Norway, Germany, and France and gave concerts in Europe accompanied by some of the most important musicians of his time. Between 1843 and 1845 he toured America from New York to San Francisco. He received enthusiastic reviews wherever he performed.

The *New York Herald* had this to say on December 4, 1845:

The unparalleled enthusiasm awakened by him everywhere, and his popularity in every city where he appeared were most remarkable. . . . He traveled more than 100,000 miles and played in every city of importance. His concerts must have given him a profit of $80,000.

Actually, he earned much more than that—an estimated $400,000 in the eastern states alone. It was an enormous sum of money for the time.

When he returned for a second tour in 1852, similar success awaited him. But this time he had other ideas as well.

Ole Bull's travels in America, with its seemingly boundless land and rich natural resources, made him increasingly aware of the poverty and miserable condition of life of many Norwegians. He felt he had to do something to help, and came up with a plan that seemed like the perfect solution. He would buy a large tract of land somewhere in America and invite poor Norwegian families to come over, settle on it, farm it, and build new, happy lives in productive labor. It was a wonderful idea that couldn't go wrong. After all, he had the money now, and what better way to spend it than in helping his poverty-stricken countrymen?

The name of this Norwegian colony would be—Oleana.

Farewell, you Mother Norway, I'm traveling far from you.
You did your best to bring me up, but it would never do.
I never had enough food—the times were always rough;
But educated people, they always had enough.

I travel 'cross the ocean unto an unknown land.
There life it will be better, as I do understand.
If we work hard once we get there, we're sure to earn our pay,
So thanks to you, Columbus, for showings us the way.[9]

It was with feelings of hope and great expectations that the first of "Ole's families" set sail from Norway in 1852 for their new life in Oleana. Norwegian newspapers had announced that Ole Bull had purchased more than 11,000 acres (4,452 hectares) of farmland in Potter County, Pennsylvania. Ole proudly stated: "We are to found a New Norway, consecrated to liberty, baptized with independence and protected by the Union's mighty flag."

Ole put his heart, soul, and money into the venture. Some three hundred houses were built, as well as a country inn, a general store, and a church. Eight hundred settlers moved in. The town of Oleana (now spelled Oleona) was born.

Ole Bornemann Bull, violin virtuoso and composer, gave concerts in Europe accompanied by some of the most important musicians of his time, such as Frederic Chopin and Franz Liszt.

Over here [in Norway] it's pretty,
But so poor, it's a pity.
While in the States it's beautiful and gold is to be found.
For here one has to settle
For so much less than little,
While there you become a millionaire before you turn around.[10]

Not quite.

It turned out that the man who sold him the land did not own it. Ole had been swindled! A short year after the enthusiastic founding of the colony, Ole Bull found himself being sued for trespassing. Lawsuit followed lawsuit. By 1854 the colony was disbanded, and the colonists were driven away by shotgun-wielding deputies. In desperation they sought new land in the Midwest, but again disaster struck. Crammed into railroad boxcars in the dead of winter, the majority of them died en route to their new destination. With the disappearance of the settlers, Ole's dream had turned into a nightmare. Oleana came to be known as "the lost colony of Oleana."

The humorous lyrics and bouncy tune of *Oleana,* poking fun at Ole Bull's venture by describing what never took place there, are in stark contrast to the reality of the situation. That often happens when songwriters take a hand in rewriting history. Facts take second place to fantasy. But then again, historians are generally not very good at writing songs.

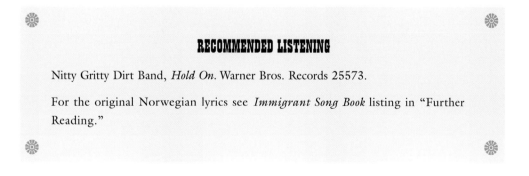

RECOMMENDED LISTENING

Nitty Gritty Dirt Band, *Hold On.* Warner Bros. Records 25573.

For the original Norwegian lyrics see *Immigrant Song Book* listing in "Further Reading."

OLEANA

English lyrics by Jerry Silverman

Music by Ditmar Meidel

In O - le - a - na, that is the place where I would stay, In - stead of bear - ing slav - 'ry's chains and suf - fer - ing in Nor - way.

Chorus

O - le, O - le - a - na, O - le, O - le - a - na,

O - le, O - le, O - le, O - le, O - le, O - le - a - na.

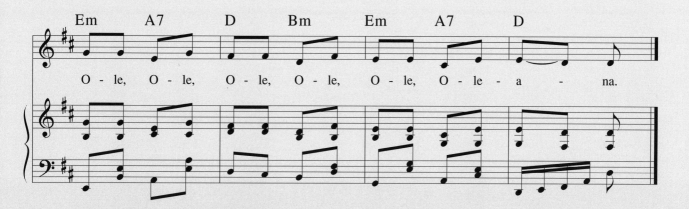

O - le, O - le, O - le, O - le, O - le, O - le - a - na.

2) In Oleana, land they'll give you,
   And it won't cost you a thing.
   Grain, it will grow by itself,
   While you just sit around and sing. *Chorus*

3) And then the grain will thresh itself
   After the harvest,
   While all I do is lie around.
   That's the part that I like best. *Chorus*

4) At the market are for sale
   The biggest spuds you e'er did see.
   Each one yields a quart of whisky
   At the distillery. *Chorus*

5) Fine Bavarian beer is here,
   As good as you have tasted.
   It runs through all the streams in town,
   And not a drop is wasted. *Chorus*

6) The salmon leap into the kettle
   Fast as they are able.
   Then they wiggle from the pot
   Right onto the table. *Chorus*

7) Rushing 'round the streets,
   Roasted piggies cause a traffic jam,
   Inquiring so politely if
   Perchance you'd like a slice of ham. *Chorus*

8) And the cows, they milk themselves.
   Please believe me, mister.
   Then they churn out cheese as good
   As does Else, my sister. *Chorus*

9) And the calves, they kill themselves
   Right before your very eyes.
   Then roast veal is served to all,
   Quicker than you realize. *Chorus*

10) The hens lay eggs so big,
    Their size surely would give you a shock.
    And the roosters strike the hour
    As well as an eight-day clock. *Chorus*

11) There's a full moon every night,
    So there is no need to grope.
    I am observing it right now—
    My bottle for a telescope. *Chorus*

12) When you go carousing,
    You'll get two dollars, and what's more,
    If you do it very well,
    They will surely give you four. *Chorus*

13) Cakes and cookies rain down
    From the heavens day and night.
    Good Lord, they are so delicious
    They're a source of great delight. *Chorus*

14) No need to support your kids,
    And to fill their purses.
    If I had to work, I couldn't
    Sit here spinning verses. *Chorus*

15) Velvet suits with silver buttons,
    We all wear without a fuss.
    And we smoke our meerschaum pipes,
    Which the old woman fills for us. *Chorus*

16) And she has to sweat and toil,
    All her work completing.
    If she doesn't finish it,
    She gives herself a beating. *Chorus*

17) Everyone plays violin,
    And dances polkas daily.
    Life is very pleasant here,
    We pass the time so gaily. *Chorus*

18) So just you go to Oleana,
    And you'll never have a care.
    The poorest wretch in Norway
    Becomes a count once over there. *Chorus*

Mississippi Song

Well, everyone is busy here, a-searching for his fortune.
For some, it seems, success is near, and they've secured their fortune.
Everyone hopes to pile it on,
La faridondaine, la faridondon,
He's off now to Mississippi.[11]

In 1719, when this French song was written, "Mississippi"—that is, Louisiana, was a French colony. It was looked upon as a potential gold mine for investors. Fortunes were made in cotton and sugarcane and furs. Fortunes were also lost in cotton and sugarcane and furs. The song continued:

It's certainly just like a trip that is called a wild goose chase,
They might as well all take a ship and search for earth out in space....

Well, as for me, I'll wait and see, here seated in my armchair,
I laugh at this activity—it's castles in the thin air....

However, by 1803, the new United States looked upon the vast Mississippi territory not as a "wild goose chase" or "castles in the thin air," but as something vital to the destiny of the nation. So it was that President Thomas Jefferson sent a delegation to France to negotiate its purchase from the French government. The French were agreeable to the idea. Napoleon, the emperor of France, was becoming more and more involved with European problems. War was in the air, and he needed the money.

The Louisiana Purchase, as it was called, transferred about 1 million square miles (2.6 million square kilometers) of territory to the

This 1865 Currier and Ives print shows the combination of bustling commerce and natural beauty that made life on the Mississippi so appealing to immigrants from harsher environments.

United States. The land included the future states of Louisiana, Missouri, Arkansas, Iowa, Minnesota, North and South Dakota, Nebraska, and Oklahoma, as well as the greater part of Kansas, Colorado, Wyoming, and Montana. The price was $27,267,622—or about four cents an acre! It was the bargain of the century. The American "West" was born.

With such a wealth of territory now opened up, land-hungry settlers from the East Coast and an ever-increasing tide of European immigrants began streaming westward. The Cumberland Gap, the soon-to-be constructed Erie Canal, as well as other overland routes, became the gateways through which thousands of families passed, seeking better lives. The National Road from Baltimore to Wheeling on the Ohio River had been opened in 1820. In 1834 the Pennsylvania Canal and Railroad was completed, linking Philadelphia and Pittsburgh by connecting the Susquehanna River to the Ohio River. Two other major east-west canals were dug between Baltimore and Cumberland, Maryland (the Chesapeake & Ohio Canal, begun in 1828 and finally completed in 1850) and between Norfolk and Buchanan, Virginia (the James River & Kanawha Canal, which took more than thirty years to construct, 1820 to 1851).

Land was not the only attraction that pulled people westward. There was that other something called *freedom*. "Out there," people felt they could breathe freely. No one would be looking over their shoulders, telling them what they could and could not do with their lives. And there was something else as well that caused people to pull up stakes and head out into the western wilderness. It was the elusive "quality of life" that beckoned. You just couldn't put your finger on it. Life was somehow just better out there. As a later song beautifully put it, people wanted "bread and roses."

As we come marching, marching, in the beauty of the day,
A million darkened kitchens, a thousand mill lofts gray
Are touched with all the radiance that a sudden sun discloses;
For the people hear us singing, "Bread and Roses, Bread and Roses." [12]

The oppressive monarchies of Europe offered little bread and no roses at all to most of their subjects. The *Mississippi Song*, which dates from 1844, tells the story from the point of view of a German immigrant who has made it to the Mississippi and is urging other Germans to join him there. Each verse of this remarkable song contains reasons why life is so much better "on the Mississippi" than back in the old country. Perhaps there was an echo of his native Rhineland, with its majestic river and fertile land, that drew him there. But it doesn't matter exactly where in the new territory the singer is. His listeners were sure to get the idea and decide for themselves just where and when to go.

The first verse rejoices in the freedom of movement in "this foreign land." No passes and no police to stop us from doing whatever we want.

Verse two expands on the idea of freedom of speech and political freedom. There is the interesting use of the French word for a policeman, *gendarme*. A beadle is a parish officer in charge of keeping order in church. Beadles had some of the functions of police and were generally not very popular figures.

Verse three turns its attention toward two oppressive aspects of life in the old country: the unfairness of the system of nobility and the official state religions that persecuted people for their differing religious beliefs. Nobility disappeared in this country with the Revolutionary War and the Declaration of Independence ("We hold these truths to be self-evident...all men are created equal..."). Official state religion disappeared with the First Amendment to the Constitution of the United States ("Congress shall make no law respecting an establishment of religion, or prohibiting the free exercise thereof...").

Verse four reminds us how bad conditions are in the old country compared with life "where our fortunes land us."

In verse five, "Michael" is informed that here his crops do not grow in support of bureaucrats [political officials] and "men of war."

Who could resist such an invitation?

There are no recordings of this song. For the original German lyrics see the *Immigrant Song Book* listing in "Further Reading."

MISSISSIPPI SONG

English lyrics by Jerry Silverman

2) Freedom of expression
   Nowhere, nowhere here
   Political repression.
   Here there's no *gendarme*
   That will give us trouble
   Here no beadle leads us
   To prison on the double—
      On the Mississippi.

3) Nobles, medal-junk,
   Title, rank and standing,
   And such stupid stuff,
   Here does find its ending.
   Here there are no priests
   Threatening hell to curb us,
   And no Jesuits
   Are here to disturb us—
      On the Mississippi.

4) Formerly we lived
   Lives of constant fearing,
   And we were like sheep
   Led unto the shearing.
   Brothers, let us go
   Where our fortunes land us.
   Singing, drinking, dancing,
   None to reprimand us—
      On the Mississippi.

5) Michael, do not sow
   Your seeds anymore now,
   For the bureaucrats
   And the men of war now.
   Michael, listen here—
   Leave with all your brothers.
   Here you're your own man,
   There you are another's—
      On the Mississippi.

Remember the Alamo!

Scots wha hae wi' Wallace bled,
Scots wham Bruce has often led,
Welcome to your gory bed,
Or to victory!
Now's the day and now's the hour,
See the front of battle lour,
See approach proud Edward's pow'r,
Chains and slavery.[13]

The great eighteenth-century Scottish poet Robert Burns wrote this song in praise of Scotland's centuries-old battles for freedom from England's rule. In particular he singled out William Wallace, who won a notable battle against English King Edward's knights in 1297, and Robert Bruce, who fought alongside Wallace and was crowned king of Scotland in 1306. The tune of this stirring song was fitted with a new set of lyrics and, as "Remember the Alamo," was first published in *The Rough and Ready Songster* in New York about 1848.

The Alamo (which got its name from the Spanish word for cottonwood tree) was an old Spanish mission in San Antonio. A grove of cottonwood trees grew along the mission's east wall.

❋

Despite the fact that Texas was part of Mexico, an increasing number of Americans began settling there in the first decades of the nineteenth century. In 1820, Moses Austin was granted a charter by the viceroy of New Spain (Mexico was a Spanish colony at that time) for the settlement of American colonists in Texas. Some three hundred American families soon arrived and began the colonization of Texas, led by Moses' son Stephen Austin.

In 1821, Mexico declared its independence from Spain. Armed conflict broke out between the mother country and its former colony, which lasted on and off for the next thirteen years. Then Mexican general Antonia Santa Anna finally took dictatorial control of the new country in 1834. Texas was officially proclaimed a state in the Mexican Republic. That's when Santa Anna's troubles really began.

The new Mexican government grew increasingly suspicious of and hostile toward the growing American population. It abolished slavery (in itself a good thing, but it angered the Texan slaveholders), levied duties and taxes, established military garrisons, and finally declared martial law and tried to disarm the Texans. "Frontier law" took over and fighting erupted. On October 2, 1835, the Mexicans were defeated at Gonzales. It was the first battle of the Texas Revolution.

By that time there were about 30,000 Americans living in Texas—four times the number of Mexicans.

In December the Mexicans were driven out of San Antonio. They agreed to withdraw to Mexico, which they did, only to return in force the following March. Under General Santa Anna, an army of more than 5,000 recaptured San Antonio and laid siege to the Alamo. The 187 Texans inside the Alamo were commanded by colonels William B. Travis and James Bowie (the developer of the "Bowie knife"). Also present was Davy Crockett, the legendary frontiersman.

On March 6, 1836, the Mexicans attacked the Alamo from all sides. Their regimental band played *Deguello* ("Cutthroat") as the troops stormed the walls. The fighting was intense, but hopeless for the Texans. All 187 perished, with the last defenders engaging in desperate hand-to-hand fighting until the end. This victory cost the Mexicans more than 1,500 lives.

> *To the memory of Crockett fill up to the brim!*
> *The hunter, the hero, the bold Yankee yeoman!*
> *Let the flowing oblation be poured forth to him,*
> *Who ne'er turned his back on his friend or his foeman.*
> *And grateful shall be*
> *His fame to the free,*
> *And forever he'll live in our fond memory.*
> *Fill! Fill! to the brave who for liberty bled—*
> *May his name and his fame to the last—Go Ahead!*[14]

(Sung to the tune of "The Star-Spangled Banner")

The Battle of the Alamo is a cornerstone of Texas history. The defenders of the old fortress all perished, but their courage inspired others to take up the call and fight for Texan independence.

The heroic defense of the Alamo by its outnumbered defenders galvanized the entire nation. Calls for revenge echoed throughout Texas and north into the United States. An army was raised under the command of General Sam Houston. The two opposing armies faced each other at the San Jacinto River, near the site of the future city of Houston, on April 21. Before the fateful battle, General Houston rallied his troops.

> The army will cross and we will meet the enemy. Some of us may be killed, must be killed; but soldiers, remember the Alamo! The Alamo! The Alamo!

Then the 783 men who comprised the entire Texan army went into battle with the cry "Remember the Alamo!" on their lips. Six hundred

Mexicans were killed and two hundred wounded in the twenty-minute battle. Nine Texans lost their lives, and thirty were wounded. The Lone Star flag of the Republic of Texas flew proudly over the land.

The Republic of Texas endured precariously for almost ten years. Then, on May 13, 1846, after a series of skirmishes between Mexican and American troops, Congress declared war against Mexico. Once again land was the issue. And once again Texas was the spark that set off the fighting, which lasted until American troops under the command of General Winfield Scott took control of Mexico City on September 13, 1847. By the terms of the Treaty of Guadalupe Hidalgo on February 2, 1848, Mexico ceded to the United States an area comprising the present states of California, Nevada, and Utah, most of Arizona and New Mexico, and parts of Wyoming and Colorado. Texas also finally joined the Union.

The westward movement of the United States had reached the Pacific Ocean.

REMEMBER THE ALAMO

Lyrics by T. A. Durriage

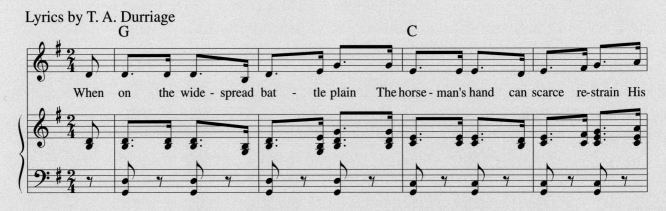

When on the wide - spread bat - tle plain The horse - man's hand can scarce re-strain His

pam - pered steed that spurns the rein, Re - mem - ber the Al - a - mo! When

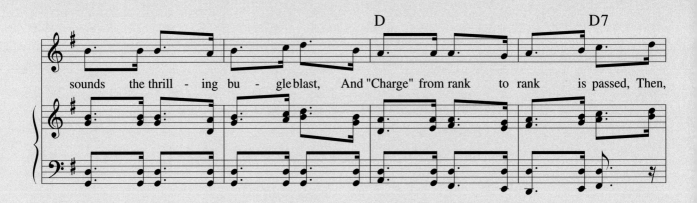

sounds the thrill - ing bu - gle blast, And "Charge" from rank to rank is passed, Then,

as your sa - bre strokes fall fast, Re - mem - ber the Al - a - mo!

2) Heed not the Spanish battle yell,
    Let every stroke we give them tell,
    And let them fall as Crockett fell.
        Remember the Alamo!
    For every wound and every thrust
    On prisoners dealt by hands accurst
    A Mexican shall bite the dust.
        Remember the Alamo!

3) The cannon's peal shall ring their knell,
    Each volley sound a passing bell,
    Each cheer Columbia's vengeance tell.
        Remember the Alamo!
    For it, disdaining flight, they stand
    And try the issue hand to hand.
    Woe to each Mexican brigand!
        Remember the Alamo!

(Sung to last 8 measures.)
    Then boot and saddle! Draw the sword!
    Unfurl your banners bright and broad,
    And as ye smite the murderous horde,
        Remember the Alamo!

Dig for the Gold

Gather 'round and I'll sing you
A little song that's sad but true,
And I'll tell you of California,
That mournful land that once I knew.
Ah, must one, then, because of gold,
Leave wife and children in the cold,
For a life of misery—
Alas! what great folly![15]

The discovery of gold at Sutter's mill on the American River near Sacramento on January 24, 1848, set into motion a frenzy of migration to California from all over the world that came to be known as the Gold Rush. In 1877 an old miner named J. H. Beadle looked back at those wild days:

> I reckon you don't remember the big excitement. No? Well it swept all Tennessee like a fire in prairie grass…. They said that men just dug gold out o' the rocks—thousands in a day…. One man said a feller dug out one lump of gold worth eight hundred thousand dollars, an' as he set on it, a feller come by with a plate o' pork an' beans, an' he offered him fifty thousand for it [the pork and beans], an' the feller stood him off for seventy-five thousand. It was in the Nashville paper, an' so every body in our parts believed it.

Stories like that drove men wild. First a trickle, then a stream, then a flood of men began beating their way to the goldfields of California. They dropped their plows, closed up their shops, kissed their wives and children good-bye, and headed west. Although some fortunes were made, most men wound up with just a few dollars to show for their labors, and others went broke. Some ended up on the wrong end of a six-shooter. Violence and lawlessness went hand in hand with the dreams of wealth that drove the men west.

This was essentially a man's world, especially in the early 1850s. In 1850 women accounted for only 2 percent of the population in the mining areas. Family life was virtually unknown. Simple basics like cooking, cleaning, and doing the laundry—tasks generally performed by women back east—posed great problems for the miners, who were too busy hunting for gold to think of much else. An incredible laundry system was organized by which the miners' dirty clothes were shipped all the way across the Pacific Ocean to Canton Province in China, where they were washed and shipped back again! This round trip took months to accomplish.

The Cantonese quickly became aware of what was going on in California, and soon an influx of Chinese men (again, no women) began arriving in San Francisco to try their luck in the mine fields. Even though the Gold Rush had attracted men from Europe as well as from all over the United States, Canada, and Mexico, the Chinese were just "too different" to be accepted on an equal basis as competing miners. Their language, dress, and customs were utterly incomprehensible to the rest of the population. Their food was "strange," they drank tea, not whisky, their religion was "heathen." In short, they didn't "belong."

They were mercilessly driven from their claims—beaten or shot if they resisted. They had come to "Golden Mountain" (that is the translation of the Cantonese word for America), but were not permitted to dig for the gold.

Oh, workmen dear, and did you hear the news that's goin' 'round?
Another China steamer has been landed in this town.
Today I read the paper and it grieved my heart full sore,
To see upon the title page, oh, just "Twelve Hundred More."

Oh, California's coming down as you can plainly see;
They are hiring all the Chinamen and discharging you and me.
But strife will be in every town throughout the Pacific shore,
And the cry of young and old shall be, "Oh, damn Twelve Hundred More!"[16]

Right: This cartoon shows the wild rush to reach California—by any means possible!

Below: Charles Christian Nahl's oil painting, entitled Sunday Morning in the Mines, *shows that a gold miners' camp was a rough and unruly place, not set up to accommodate women or children.*

Ironically, this anti-Chinese song was sung to the tune of the Irish patriotic ballad "The Wearing of the Green," which lamented British anti-Irish policies in the eighteenth century.

Denied the right to mine, the Chinese turned to what they were permitted to do, what they did well, and what did not compete with the miners: cooking and washing clothes—two extremely necessary occupations at the time. And so the "American institutions" of the Chinese restaurant and Chinese laundry were born.

There are no recordings of this song. For other songs of Chinese immigrants in California see the *Immigrant Song Book* in "Further Reading."

DIG FOR THE GOLD

By Charlie Chin

I was on - ly a boy in old Can - ton town, When I

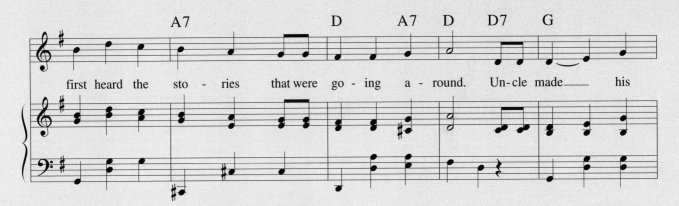

first heard the sto - ries that were go - ing a - round. Un - cle made____ his

for - tune, and he wore a gold ring. If you asked him a - bout it, he

glad - ly would sing. "Dig for the gold, dig for the

gold. I'll be a rich man in Chi-na be-fore I grow old."

2) Well, I boarded a ship, it was all made of wood.
   The bedding was lousy and the food was no good.
   Six companies met us on Frisco's long pier—
   Of three hundred started, only two hundred here. *Chorus*

3) Well, I walked to the hills my fortune to find,
   Of hardship and want, well, I paid it no mind.
   But the jumpers were waiting, and they wished us all dead.
   They took all our claims and put lumps on our head. *Chorus*

4) Well, I headed for Hangtown, the biggest of camps,
   There was gambling and murder by the light of the lamps.
   Of the money I had, it was gone in a wink,
   I spent it on women and foul whisky drink. *Chorus*

5) Brandy Gulch was my next stop, but who should I meet,
   But a crazy old miner they called One-Eyed Pete.
   I picked up a six-gun and put down the spade—
   By robbing and killing our fortune was made. *Chorus*

6) Vigilantes, they caught us at the place called Pig Hill.
   Old Pete with a hangnoose the miners did kill.
   They banged me and beat me 'til they thought I was dead
   But I lived 'til the morning and I ran off instead. *Chorus*

7) Well, I ran to the place where we hid all our loot,
   I bought me some new clothes and a pair of new boots.
   Took a trip back to China on the next swelling tide—
   When they asked me about it, I turned and I lied.

   Last chorus:
   It was digging for gold, digging for gold,
   I was a rich man in China before I grew old.

Banks of
the Sacramento

'Round Cape Horn where the stiff winds blow,
'Round Cape Horn where there's sleet and snow.[17]

Cape Horn is the name given to the southernmost tip of South America, where the Atlantic and Pacific oceans meet. Rounding the Cape, with its swirling currents, gale force winds, thick fogs, and occasional icebergs had been the terror of sailors since the first explorations in the sixteenth century. It was, however, the only way to get to the Orient by sailing west across the Atlantic. The Portuguese navigator Ferdinand Magellan was the first to pass through the strait, a narrow passage, 360 miles (580 kilometers) long, which now bears his name, on November 28, 1520. His expedition of small sailing vessels was the first to circumnavigate the globe. He himself never made it all the way. He was killed on April 27, 1521, in a battle on Matacan, an island in the Philippines, while attempting to conquer it for "God and country."

By the middle of the nineteenth century, sailing ships engaged in the China tea trade were regularly rounding Cape Horn on their journeys from England and America to the Far East. By 1830 a new type of fast sailing vessel, the clipper ship, was being developed. Clippers were built for speed; the fragile tea leaves tended to spoil in the hulls of the slow-moving older sailing ships. The new design caught on, and soon shipyards in Boston, New York, Baltimore, and England were launching faster and faster clippers—just in time to begin transporting eager adventurers to the gold diggings "on the banks of the Sacramento."

In 1848 the clipper *Sea Witch* sailed from Canton, China, to New York in a record seventy-seven days. Two years later she sailed the 18,000 miles (29,000 kilometers) from New York to San Francisco in ninety-seven days. The older sailing vessels of the time took up to five months to make the passage. The *Sea Witch's* time was handily beaten by the Boston-built clipper *Flying Cloud* on April 9, 1852, when she arrived in San Francisco eighty-nine days and twenty hours after leaving New York. Then, on April 20, 1854, the never-to-be-beaten record was established by the *Flying Cloud;* after leaving her berth at the foot of Maiden Lane in New York, she dropped anchor after completing the journey in eighty-nine days and eight hours—seventeen days faster than the next best time posted by another clipper, the *Archer.*

This woodcut advertising the "great beauty of model" of the Flying Cloud, *was made in the hope of attracting passengers two years before the ship's record-breaking trip to San Francisco.*

Once in San Francisco, the gold hunters were surprised to find that so many others were in search of the same dream. This is an 1849 etching of San Francisco's harbor, jammed with ships.

The clipper ships caught the imagination of thousands of gold seekers, especially those who could afford the price of a ticket. During all of 1848 about half a dozen vessels ventured around the Cape to San Francisco Bay. The next year saw the number leap to more than 700, carrying more than 90,000 passengers. Over the next three years at least one fast clipper was always docked in New York, loading day and night with supplies and people bound for San Francisco. As tens of thousands of hopeful gold seekers debarked, even the crews deserted many of the ships to join in the mad rush to strike it rich. Who needed to risk one's life on the high seas on a seaman's miserable pay (sailing 'round the stormy Cape to boot), when "instant wealth" lay there for the taking in your pan or at the end of your pick? Indeed, often enough the crew was composed of an unwholesome mixture of men who had either been "shanghaied" (dragged on board while drunk or drugged) or who had signed on merely to get a free trip to the gold-fields. As a result of these mass desertions, there were so many abandoned ships clogging the port of San Francisco that a great number of them were converted into waterfront stores, hotels, and saloons.

Banks of the Sacramento was widely sung on board ship and on land. It was popular not only because of its lyrics, which told a story that everyone who had been to California, was on the way to California, or was in California could relate to—but also because of its tune, the well-known *Camptown Races* by Stephen Foster.

RECOMMENDED LISTENING

How the West Was Won. Rhino Records 72458.

The Chrysanthemum Ragtime Band. *Preserves,* Vol. 1. Omega 3011.

BANKS OF THE SACRAMENTO

Music by Stephen Foster ("Camptown Races")

In the Black Ball Line I served my time, With a hoo-dah, With a

hoo-dah; In a full-rigged ship, and in her prime, with a hoo-dah,— hoo-dah

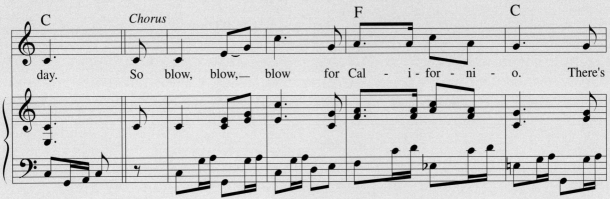

day. So blow, blow,— blow for Cal-i-for-ni-o. There's

plen-ty of gold, so I've been told, On the banks of the Sac-ra-men-to.

2) A bully ship and a bully crew,
   Hoo-dah, to me hoo-dah,
   A bully mate and a captain, too,
   Hoo-dah, hoo-dah day. *Chorus*

3) Round Cape Horn in the months of snows,
   Hoo-dah, to me hoo-dah,
   If we get there nobody knows,
   Hoo-dah, hoo-dah day. *Chorus*

   Similarly
4) Oh, around the Horn with a mainsail set,
   Around Cape Horn and we're all wringing wet.

5) Oh, around Cape Horn in the month of May,
   Oh, around Cape Horn is a very long way.

6) To the Sacramento we're bound away,
   To the Sacramento's a hell of a way.

7) Oh, a bully ship with a bully crew,
   But the mate is a bastard through and through.

8) Ninety days to 'Frisco Bay,
   Ninety days is damn good pay.

9) Sing and heave and heave and sing,
   Heave and make them handspikes ring.

10) I wish to God I'd never been born,
    To go a-rambling around Cape Horn.

Paddy Works on the Railway

Oh, the praties they grow small over here, over here.
Oh, the praties they grow small over here.
Oh, the praties they grow small and we dig them in the fall,
And we eat them skin and all, over here, over here.[18]

In the 1840s a terrible famine swept across Ireland. In 1844 the staple food crop, the potato ("pratie") was attacked by a blight that soon made itself felt with devastating results. Crop after crop failed. The winter of 1846–1847 was the most severe that people could remember. There were great icy gales blowing snow, hail, and sleet. What the Irish at the time called "the Starvation" was partial in 1845, general in 1846, and universal in 1847. Uncounted hundreds of thousands of people died (estimates range from 200,000 to 1,000,000). A great exodus began "across the western ocean" to "Americay." They arrived in increasing numbers in Boston and New York—up to a million in the 1850s, looking for hope, looking for a chance to start over, to make a living.

Many found that chance a-working on the railway.

※

December 1830 marks the beginning of the age of steam railroading in the United States. That was the year that the South Carolina Railroad's locomotive, *The Best Friend of Charleston,* pulled a string of coaches out on its inaugural run out of Charleston. By 1833 some 135 miles (217 kilometers) of track had been laid through cotton country in the general direction of Augusta, Georgia. The nation was quick to realize the enormous economic potential of railroad trains. They could haul freight and passengers faster, farther, and more efficiently than any other means of transportation yet invented. And that included the canals that had recently been built and would still continue to be built for some time to come.

In 1833 the 1,000,000 square miles (1,600,000 square kilometers) of the Louisiana Purchase of 1803 were still largely unexplored and uninhabited. It took weeks for the slow, lumbering covered wagons (sometimes called "prairie schooners," comparing them to slow-moving sailing ships) to travel the thousands of miles across that vast, uncharted, wild territory. Roads were nonexistent, rivers were difficult to cross, the weather was unpredictable, food was always a problem, and hostile Indians posed an ever-present threat.

And beyond the Louisiana Territory loomed the Rocky Mountains, California, and the Pacific Ocean. Could the age-old dream of "sailing" west (in prairie schooners) to get to the Pacific finally be realized? Could a railroad cross the continent, linking the Atlantic and the Pacific?

Before that question was finally answered, thirty-six years of intense railroad-building gripped the nation. Some of the first tracks were laid alongside the canals, slowly squeezing the life out of them. Twenty-five years after the opening of the Erie Canal, three railroads ran parallel to that waterway.

In the thirty-one years between the first run of *The Best Friend of Charleston* and the outbreak of the Civil War in 1861, railroad lines were laid up and down the eastern seaboard, linking major cities and small towns, and gradually pushing westward.

As new states were added to the Union the need for east-west rail transportation became increasingly obvious. And with the discovery of gold in California in 1848, a whole new urgency was added to the question of railroading in America. In 1848 the population of California was about 15,000. In 1850, California was admitted as the thirty-first state. By 1852 the census counted 223,856 Californians. How did they all get there?

Most had literally walked across the continent—a dangerous journey that took weeks or months, depending on luck. How many never made it all the way—turned back or died along the trails—can never be known. Others, as we have seen, sailed the perilous route around the tip of South America—Cape Horn, known for its treacherous cur-

The Chicago & Alton railway line promoted the luxury of cross-country Pullman cars that allowed for sleeping and dining en route—a far cry from the ox-drawn wagons of the pre-railroad era.

rents, violent storms, and shipwrecks. Still others sailed down to Panama and struggled through the disease-infested jungle to the Pacific Ocean, where they boarded another ship for the trip to San Francisco.

There was no question that what was needed was a railroad connecting California with the rest of the Union. That much was obvious. But where and how to build it posed enormous problems. No engineering project on such grand a scale had ever been attempted before.

With the outbreak of the Civil War, the building of the transcontinental railway became a military matter of great national urgency. Union troops would need to be transported quickly over ever-increasing distances. The first surveying of the projected route for the Central Pacific Railroad over the mountains from Sacramento began in the summer of 1861. Groundbreaking took place on January 8, 1863. That was the easy part.

The hard part soon became apparent.

First of all, practically every piece of equipment—including rails and locomotives had to be shipped from northern East Coast ports around Cape Horn. That 18,000-mile (29,000-kilometer) journey could take anywhere from five to eight months.

Blasting and tunneling through mountains with primitive gunpowder, and clearing away the debris with shovels and wheelbarrows, posed unimaginable difficulties. Snows in the High Sierras frequently buried the newly laid tracks. Then there was the problem of getting enough workers to keep the job moving along. The Union Army had first call on able-bodied young men. So the bulk of the heavy work was done by Chinese laborers who had come to California seeking gold, only to be driven out of the mines and off their claims by racial discrimination. There were 20,000 Chinese living in California in 1864. By 1865 more than 10,000 of them were working on the railway. When even this number proved insufficient, another 7,000 to 12,000 laborers were imported from China.

The groundbreaking for the westbound tracks of the Union Pacific Railroad commenced at Omaha, Nebraska, on December 2, 1863. On the Great Plains, the mostly Irish workforce did not face the terrible difficulties that were a daily fact of life on the California side. The two lines were to meet up at Promontory Point, a desolate spot near Ogden, Utah.

With the end of the Civil War in 1865 the labor shortage was considerably eased. Thousands of discharged soldiers, Northern and Southern, looking for work and used to roughing it in the outdoors, flocked to railroad building. The approaching lines moved closer and closer.

When the golden spike was driven into the final railroad tie joining the two lines on May 10, 1869, a one-word message was telegraphed back to Washington: DONE.

And done it was. An iron ribbon of track joined the Atlantic and Pacific, setting the stage for the next great chapter in American history—the settling of the West.

RECOMMENDED LISTENING

Barley Bree, *The Best of Barley Bree*. Shanachie Records 52039.

Songs Of Ireland. Mandacy Records 8718.

PADDY WORKS ON THE RAILWAY

In eight-een hun-dred and for-ty one, I put my cor-du-roy brit-ches on, I

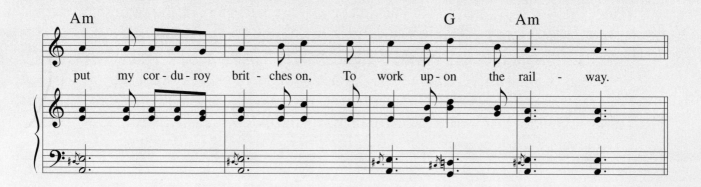

put my cor-du-roy brit-ches on, To work up-on the rail - way.

Chorus

Fil - i - mi-oo - ri-oo - ri-ay, Fil - i - mi-oo - ri-oo - ri-ay,

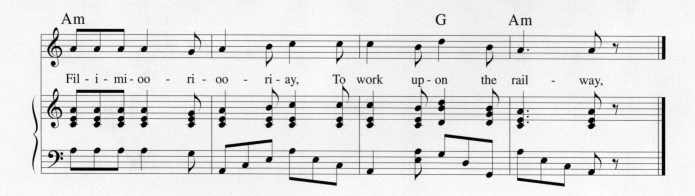

Fil - i - mi-oo - ri-oo - ri-ay, To work up-on the rail - way,

2) In eighteen hundred and forty-two,
   I left the old world for the new,
   Bad cess to the luck that brought me through,
   To work upon the railway. *Chorus*

3) In eighteen hundred and forty-three,
   'Twas then I met sweet Biddy McGee,
   An elegant wife she's been to me,
   While working on the railway. *Chorus*

4) In eighteen hundred and forty-four,
   I worked again, and worked some more,
   It's "Bend your backs," the boss did roar,
   While working on the railway. *Chorus*

5) It's "Pat, do this," and "Pat, do that,"
   Without a stocking or cravat,
   And nothing but an old straw hat,
   While working on the railway. *Chorus*

6) In eighteen hundred and forty-five,
   They worked us worse than bees in a hive,
   I didn't know if I was dead or alive,
   While working on the railway. *Chorus*

7) In eighteen hundred and forty-six,
   They pelted me with stones and sticks,
   Oh, I was in a terrible fix,
   While working on the railway. *Chorus*

8) In eighteen hundred and forty-seven,
   Sweet Biddy McGee, she went to heaven.
   If she left one child, she left eleven,
   To work upon the railway. *Chorus*

Sweet Betsy
from Pike

There was a rich merchant in London did dwell,
He had but one daughter, an uncommon fine young gal,
Her name it was Dinah, just sixteen years old,
With a very large fortune in silver and gold.[19]

There was probably not one person in the entire English-speaking world of the mid- to late-nineteenth century who was not familiar with the British music hall comic ballad "Villikins and His Dinah," which describes the tragic fates of young Dinah and her lover Villikins.

When this song crossed the Atlantic it was taken up by singers—professional and amateur, on stage and off. It was not only the words that captured the popular imagination (Dinah rejects her father's demand that she not marry Villikins, and the lovers, true to Shakespearean tradition, commit suicide), but the delightful tune, which over the years has been borrowed many times to carry new and different lyrics.

Transplanted to America, the lovers took on new identities as Betsy and Ike, while their adventures took them—where else?—to California.

The life of the California miner was not all work and no play. Life would have been unbearable if it had not offered some diversions. Gambling and drinking "palaces" sprang up all over San Francisco in the 1850s. While much of the miners' money was evaporating at the gambling tables, and the rotgut whisky was flowing freely, there was music in the air —in the saloons, hotels, inns, and, of course, the music halls. Writing in 1850, one observer of the scene noted: "These songs are universally popular, and the crowd of listeners is often so great, as to embarrass the player at the monte tables and injure the business of the gamblers."[20]

Responding to this universal desire for musical entertainment, a new breed of Californian came into being: the goldfield minstrel and songwriter. Composing and singing songs about miners for the miners, these professional entertainers enjoyed tremendous success. They knew whereof they sang, for many of them had come west seeking gold dust themselves. And like the proprietors of establishments where they held forth nightly, they recognized a need and filled it.

Perhaps no other singer-songwriter captured the spirit of the time better than a colorful character by the name of John A. Stone. He had gone west in 1850, part of that great flood of humanity in search of El Dorado, the fabled golden land of the earlier Spanish explorers. Coming up empty-handed after three years of fruitless digging, he turned to composing and singing. Under the name of "Old Put," he literally became the singing voice of the Gold Rush, turning out more than fifty songs between 1853 and 1858.

He organized a traveling minstrel company known as "The Sierra Nevada Rangers," which toured the miners' camps, entertaining the miners and earning its pay in gold dust. His success proved that there was more than one way to get gold out of the ground.

In 1855, at the height of his popularity, Stone published a collection of some of his best-known songs in a volume entitled *Put's Original California Songster*. Writing about himself and his songs (in the third person), Stone offered these thoughts in the preface to the book:

> Many of his songs show some hard edges, and he is free to confess that they may fail to please the more aristocratic portion of the community who have but little sympathy with the details, hopes, trials or joys of the toiling miner's life; but he is confident that the class he addresses will not find them exaggerated, nothing extenuated, nor aught set down "in malice."

The *Songster* had a phenomenal success. More than 15,000 copies were sold in a few years, and in 1858, Stone brought out another collection of original pieces, *Put's Golden Songster*. The adventures of "Sweet Betsy From Pike" are recounted for the first time in print in this 1858 edition.

Stone was clever enough to set Betsy's transcontinental exploits to a tune that everyone already knew, "Villikins and His Dinah," thus assuring that his listeners would at least be humming it after a first hearing. Then, to learn the words (since the average miner certainly could not read music), all they would have to do was purchase a copy of *Put's Golden Songster*, which was conveniently on sale after each performance.

The narrative of the song follows a trail with which each and every miner was guaranteed to be familiar. Even though not everyone started out, as Betsy and Ike did, from Pike County, Missouri, or camped somewhere on the Platte River, as it meandered through Salt Lake City on the way to California, enough of them had followed a route similar enough for the tale to ring true. For example, between the time of the discovery of gold in January 1848 and July 1851, some 40,000 people and their 10,000 wagons had passed through

Crossing the wide prairies with two yoke of oxen was a real adventure for families such as Sweet Betsy and Ike...but the real test came with crossing over the Rocky Mountains.

Fort Laramie, Wyoming, a major trading post on the Platte River on their way west.

It was no wonder that the journey of "Sweet Betsy From Pike" was a shared experience between singer and listener—a surefire formula for a hit song.

RECOMMENDED LISTENING

Mormon Tabernacle Choir, *This Is Your Land.* CBS Masterworks 06747.

Great American String Band, *200 Years of American Heritage.* C.M.H. Productions 1776.

Riders in the Sky, *Saddle Pals.* Rounder Records 8011.

Disneyland Cast, *Children's Favorites.* Disney 60607.

SWEET BETSY FROM PIKE

Lyrics by John A. Stone

Music: "Villikins And His Dinah"

Did you ev - er hear tell of sweet Bet - sy from Pike, Who

crossed the wide prai - ries with her lov - er, Ike; With two yoke of

ox - en and one spot - ted hog, A— tall shang - hai roos - ter, an old yel - low

Chorus

dog? Sing— too - ral - i, oo - ral - i, oo - ral - i - ay.

2) The shanghai ran off and their cattle all died,
That morning the last piece of bacon was fried;
Poor Ike was discouraged and Betsy got mad,
The dog drooped his tail and looked wondrously sad. *Chorus*

3) They stopped at Salt Lake to inquire the way
When Brigham declared that sweet Betsy should stay;
But Betsy got frightened and ran like a deer,
While Brigham stood pawing the ground like a steer. *Chorus.*

4) They soon reached the desert, where Betsy gave out,
And down in the sand she lay rolling about;
While Ike, half distracted, looked on with surprise,
Saying. "Betsy, get up, you'll get sand in your eyes." *Chorus*

5) Sweet Betsy got up in a great deal of pain,
Declared she'd go back to Pike County again;
But Ike gave a sigh, and they fondly embraced,
And they traveled along with his arm 'round her waist. *Chorus*

6) One evening quite early they camped on the Platte,
'Twas near by the road on a green shady flat,
Where Betsy, sore-footed, lay down to repose,
With wonder Ike gazed on that Pike County rose. *Chorus*

7) Their wagons broke down with a terrible crash,
And out on the prairie rolled all kinds of trash;
A few little baby clothes done up with care,
'Twas rather suspicious, though all on the *square. Chorus*

8) They suddenly stopped on a very high hill,
With wonder looked down upon old Placerville;
Ike sighed when he said, and he cast his eyes down,
"Sweet Betsy, my darling, we've got to Hangtown." *Chorus*

9) Long Ike and sweet Betsy attended a dance;
Ike wore a pair of his Pike County pants;
Sweet Betsy was covered with ribbons and rings;
Says Ike, "You're an angel, but where are your wings?"

10) A miner said, "Betsy, will you dance with me?"
"I will that, old hoss, if you don't make too free;
But don't dance me hard, do you want to know why?
Dog on you, I'm chock full of strong alkali!" *Chorus*

11) This Pike County couple got married of course,
But Ike became jealous, obtained a divorce;
Sweet Betsy, well satisfied, said with a great shout,
"Good-by, you big lummox, I'm glad you've backed out."

The Old Chisholm Trail

Whoopy ti yi yi, get along, little dogies,
It's your misfortune, and none of my own,
Whoopy ti yi yi, get along, little dogies,
For you know that Wyoming will be your new home.[21]

In order for the "little dogies" (stray calves) to get to their "new home" in Wyoming from their old home in Texas, they had to be driven up the Western Trail through Oklahoma, Kansas, Nebraska, and Colorado. The Western Trail was but one of a number of cattle trails over which the cowboys drove their herds of longhorn steers north either to new grazing ranges or to the stockyards, slaughterhouses, and railroads of the Midwest.

The Western Trail originated at Bandera, Texas, and crossed the Atchison, Topeka & Santa Fe Railroad at Dodge City, Kansas. From there it continued north to Ogallala, Nebraska, where it crossed the North Platte River and the tracks of the Union Pacific Railroad. Passing through Wyoming, it led into Montana, where it passed over the tracks of the Northern Pacific and terminated at the tracks of the Great Northern Railroad, not far from the Canadian border. This alternating between open prairie and railroad yards gave the herds ample time to fatten up before being converted into steaks and hamburgers.

To the east of the Western Trail lay the Shawnee Trail, which began in San Antonio. The Shawnee split into two forks at Shawnee, Oklahoma. One branch curved northwestward to Abilene, Kansas. The eastern branch continued on to Kansas City.

Lying more or less midway between the Western Trail and the Shawnee Trail, heading due north from San Antonio to Abilene, was the Chisholm Trail.

It was no accident that south Texas was the birthplace of the cowboy—the great symbol of the American West. In order for this "birth" to come about, five necessary ingredients had to be present in just the right proportions: grass, water, cattle, horses, and men. With San Antonio as its northernmost point, the first great cattle range stretched south to Laredo on the Mexican border, southeast along the Rio Grande to Brownsville on the Gulf of Mexico, from there up the coast to the ghost town of Indianola (near present-day Bay City) and back again to San Antonio.

When Texas gained its independence from Mexico in 1836, and the new American Texans took over the country north of the Rio Grande, they took over as well the herds of longhorns—cattle so wild that only a man on horseback dared approach them. The Mexican *vaquero* (cowboy) had mastered the techniques of handling cattle on horseback. He could handle horse, rope, saddle, spur, and branding iron. The Texans learned their lessons fast and well and soon were masters of horse, cattle, and range.

Jesse Chisholm (c. 1806–1868) was a Scottish-Cherokee trader and rancher in the Oklahoma Indian Territory, whose wagon wheels broke part of the trail that would eventually bear his name. He often traveled from a trading post on the north fork of the Canadian River north to trade with the Wichita Indians on the Washita River in Kansas, a distance of 220 miles (354 kilometers). That was Jesse's as-yet unnamed trail.

In the decades immediately preceding the Civil War, the raising of livestock had not yet become big business. The end of the war, as we have seen, ushered in the era of the railroad, with new lines leading to both coasts. Now beef could be transported easily to the hungry markets of the East and very soon to feed the exploding population of the West. The cattlemen needed the railways, and the railways needed the cattle.

In 1867 a cattle depot was established in Abilene, a small town on the brand-new Union Pacific Railroad. Texas cattlemen saw their chance

The Chisholm Trail and cowboys who traveled it are celebrated in many songs, but life on the trail was more lonesome than it was romantic. They chose the route because it had no hills or settlements — an advantage for the moving cattle, but not for their keepers.

to expand their market, and soon thousands of cattle were being driven by hundreds of cowboys up Jesse Chisholm's old wagon trail. The Chisholm Trail was born.

In 1871, the peak year, the trail resounded to the hooves of a record 600,000 cattle heading north. Individual herds numbered in the hundreds, with twenty or thirty cowboys per herd driving them along. The trail outfit also included six or eight horses to a man, chuck wagons (traveling kitchens) and all the supplies needed to sustain the men on the ride, which might cover as much as 800 miles (1,300 kilometers) at the leisurely pace of 10 miles (16 kilometers) a day—if the going was good. The many rivers and streams encountered along the way slowed everything down until the herd was regrouped on the northern banks.

By the 1880s a new obstacle to the cattle drives presented itself that could not easily be overcome: barbed-wire fences. The conflict between the cowboy and the farmer was one that the cowboy, for all his strength and courage, could not win. The land was simply becoming fenced in. Big agriculture was in direct competition for space with the cowboy and his herd. (In the 1943 Broadway musical *Oklahoma*, the chorus sings "The cowboy and the farmer should be friends...." A hit song of 1944 was the nostalgic "Don't Fence Me In.")

❋

"The Old Chisholm Trail" was the "hit song" of the 1870s. It starts out with the age-old ballad singer's invitation to "listen to my tale," and proceeds through literally hundreds of simple two-line verses to tell the tale of every adventure and misadventure that befell the cowboys and their cattle along the way. It is as long as the trail itself. The cowboys sang it to themselves to relieve boredom and stay awake in the saddle. They sang it to each other, trading verses made up on the spot. They sang it to calm their nervous, skittish longhorns.

RECOMMENDED LISTENING

Tex Ritter, *The Cowboy Album*. Kid Rhino 70403.

Wayne Erbsen, *Cowboy Songs of the Wild Frontier*. Native Ground Music 400.

Michael Martin Murphy, *Cowboy Songs*. Warner Bros. Records 26308.

VIDEO Country Sing-Along. Warner Alliance 38409.

THE OLD CHISHOLM TRAIL

Well, come a - long, boys, and lis - ten to my tale, and I'll

Chorus

tell you of my trou - bles on the old Chis - holm Trail. Come - a

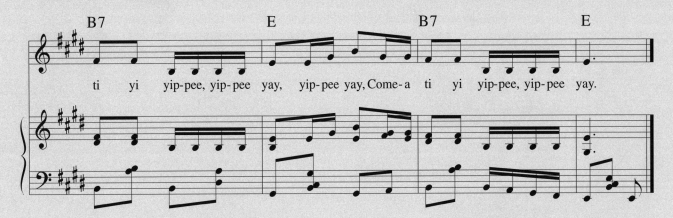

ti yi yip - pee, yip - pee yay, yip - pee yay, Come - a ti yi yip - pee, yip - pee yay.

2) I started up the trail October twenty-third,
   I started up the trail with the 2-U herd. *Chorus*

3) I jumped in the saddle and grabbed a-holt the horn,
   Best durn cowboy ever was born. *Chorus*

4) I'm up in the morning before daylight
   And before I sleep, the moon shines bright. *Chorus*

5) It's bacon and beans 'most every day,
   I'd as soon been a-eating prairie hay. *Chorus*

6) Cloudy in the east and it looks like rain,
   And my damned old slicker's in the wagon again. *Chorus*

7) Wind began to blow—rain began to fall,
   It looked, by grab, like we was gonna loose 'em all. *Chorus*

8) A heifer went loco and the boss said, "Kill it."
   I shot it in the arse with the handle of a skillet. *Chorus*

9) I went to the boss to draw my roll.
   He had me figgered out nine dollars in the hole. *Chorus*

10) So me and the boss, we had a little chat.
    I hit him in the face with my big slouch hat. *Chorus*

11) So the boss said to me, "I'm gonna fire you—
    "And not only you but the whole damn crew." *Chorus*

12) Well, I'm going back home to draw my money,
    Going back home to see my honey. *Chorus*

13) On a ten-dollar hoss and a forty-dollar saddle,
    I'm a-going to punch them Texas cattle. *Chorus*

14) Well my feet are in the stirrup and my saddle's in the sky,
    And I'll quit punching cows in the Sweet Bye and Bye. *Chorus*

 Home on the Range

Then come along, come along, make no delay,
Come from every nation, come from every way;
Our lands they are broad enough, don't be alarmed,
For Uncle Sam is rich enough to give us all a farm.[22]

Railroads were being built, canals were being dug, gold was being panned, and cowboys were hitting the long trails—but one ingredient was missing in the mix. The Louisiana Purchase had virtually doubled the size of the United States in 1803; the war with Mexico had added the southwest to our territory in 1848. The map was almost complete. But where were the people needed to fill up this enormous empty territory? The land cried out for settlers—families that would plow, plant, and harvest; build homes and future cities; and fulfill the promise of America.

❈

Ever since 1785, the policy of the United States government had supported the idea that the public domain (unsettled public land) belonged to the people, and that each family was entitled to a home or farm. The initial result of this policy was that speculators bought up large tracts of land in the thirteen original states, which were then offered for sale to those who could pay the price. This was not exactly what the government had in mind. Poor immigrants could hardly afford to become landowners under these conditions.

As the frontier gradually pushed westward, some attempt to relieve this situation took place in 1841, when the government offered public domain land for sale west of the Appalachians at $1.25 an acre. This was not, however, the "free land" that many had hoped for, and over the next twenty years a number of "homestead bills," designed to give some relief to prospective settlers, were introduced in Congress.

Then, on May 20, 1862, with the Civil War raging, President Lincoln signed into law the Homestead Act. It provided that any citizen, or alien who had declared the intention of becoming a citizen, on payment of $10 could file a claim for up to 160 acres (65 hectares). A further condition stipulated that after having "resided upon or cultivated" that land for the following five years, the settler could receive permanent title to the land.

But it wasn't always easy.

> *I am looking rather seedy now while holding down my claim,*
> *And my vittles are not always of the best;*
> *And the mice play shyly 'round me as I nestle down to rest*
> *In my little old sod shanty on the plain.*
> *Oh, the hinges are of leather and the windows have no glass,*
> *While the roof it lets the howling blizzard in.*
> *And I hear the hungry coyote as he slinks up through the grass*
> *'Round my little old sod shanty on the plain.*[23]

There were no forests on the plains, no trees to provide lumber for the simplest log cabin, let alone farmhouse and barn. Even the building of fences posed problems. The "little old sod shanty" was often just a dugout with an earthen roof, a roof that dripped water for days after a rain. When it rained, that is. One worn-out farmer said: "In God we trusted, in Kansas we busted...what with sand storms, cyclones, dry weather, blizzards and grasshoppers...."

Another homesteader put it this way: "I've got a little bet with the government. They're betting me I can't live here for five years, and I'm betting them that I can."

> *At first we made some money here,*
> *With drought and grasshoppers each year;*
> *But now the interest that we pay*
> *Soon takes our money all away.*[24]

Some homesteaders lost the bet, but most won it.

The range did indeed become "home" as wagons and stagecoaches and then trains brought more and more people to the new frontier. In this John Gast painting, American Progress, *an angelic woman guides the pioneers. She is carrying a book of knowledge and stringing telegraph wires in her wake. Farms, technology, and a new civilization follow closely behind, but a careful viewing shows that progress has its price: the Native Americans are directly in the path of "Progress" and are in danger of being trampled.*

Despite all the hardships, the loneliness, the uncertainties, and the backbreaking labor, the crops grew and the land prospered. The railroads, in whose interest it was to see the land populated, spread their networks throughout the new territories. They printed glowing advertisements and posters that they hoped would entice families to move out west and start a new life on "Uncle Sam's farm." That people responded to this "general invitation to the people of the world" is amply proven by the fact that during the forty-year period immediately following the Homestead Act, 718,930 homesteads, comprising 96,495,414 acres (39,051,694 hectares) were established.

In 1873 a prairie doctor named Higley Brewster, of Smith County, Kansas, whose medical office and home was a typical dugout, looked about him and recognized the beauty of the land. He was so moved by his emotions that he wrote a poem, which when set to music by Daniel E. Kelly, became the most famous of all Western songs—"Home on the Range."

RECOMMENDED LISTENING

Gene Autry, *Western Classics*. Columbia 09001.

Bing Crosby, *My Favorite Country Songs*. MCA Special Products 20982.

Pete Seeger, *Cowboy Songs From Folkways*. Folkways/Smithsonian 40043.

HOME ON THE RANGE

Lyrics by Higley Brewster

Music by Daniel E. Kelly

Oh, give me a home where the buf - fa - lo roam, Where the

deer and the an - te - lope play;_____ Where

sel - dom is heard a dis - cour - ag - ing word, And the

skies are not clou - dy all day._____

Home, home on the range, Where the deer and the

an - te - lope play; Where sel - dom is heard a dis-

cour - ag - ing word, And the skies are not cloud - y all day.

2) Oh! give me land where the bright diamond sand
Throws its light from the glittering streams,
Where glideth along the graceful white swan,
Like the maid to her heavenly dreams. *Chorus*

3) How often at night, when the heavens were bright,
With the light of the twinkling stars,
Have I stood here amazed and asked as I gazed
If their glory exceeds that of ours. *Chorus*

4) I love the wild flowers in this bright land of ours,
I love the wild curlew's shrill scream;
The bluffs and white rocks and antelope flocks,
That graze on the mountain so green. *Chorus*

5) The air is so pure and the breezes so free,
The zephyrs so balmy and light,
That I would not exchange my home here to range
Forever in azures so bright. *Chorus*

Acres of Clams

I'm gonna hit that Oregon Trail this comin' fall.
I'm gonna hit that Oregon Trail this comin' fall.
Where the good rain falls a-plenty and the crops and orchards grow—
I'm gonna hit that Oregon Trail this comin' fall.[25]

One more major piece of the jigsaw puzzle was needed to complete the country's map. Starting near Independence, Missouri, the 2,000-mile (3,200-kilometer) Oregon Trail wound its way through Kansas, along the Platte River in Nebraska, on through Wyoming's North Platte River country, along the Sweetwater River and through the south pass in the continental divide into Utah. (The continental divide is the line of summits of the Rocky Mountains, separating streams flowing toward the Pacific from those flowing toward the Gulf of Mexico, Hudson Bay, and the Arctic Ocean.) From there the trail split, with one branch heading south to California and the other following the Snake River through the Grande Ronde Valley and over the Blue Mountains until the travelers reached the mighty Columbia River, which flows between Washington and Oregon.

The trail was a difficult one, with many rivers, mountains, and stretches of desert to cross. Covered wagons, drawn by oxen, horses, or mules, could take anywhere from four to six months to make the trip from Independence to the Columbia River. In some places, the ruts made by the wagons are still visible to this day.

❊

In their vain quest for the mythical Northwest Passage, which would allow ships to sail west from Europe to China and India, Spanish navigators first sighted the Oregon shore in 1543. The Pacific Ocean had already been discovered, and these Spanish ships were hoping to find a way back home without having to sail around Cape Horn. Of course, they didn't find it—it doesn't exist.

Spanish exploration continued up and down the coast over the next two hundred years, and in 1775, Spain took formal possession of the northwest coast. By 1778 ships of the British Royal Navy began sailing along the Oregon coast, trading for sea otter skins with the Indians. This led to an increase of commerce between this northwest region, England, and China. The Americans entered this lucrative trade market in 1789. Three years later, the American captain Robert Gray sailed for the first time up a broad river, which he named in honor of his ship, *Columbia*.

With Great Britain and the United States both having established trading posts in the Oregon country, trouble was bound to arise as to what belonged to whom. British Canada was just to the north; the United States was slowly but surely pushing westward. Spain was more concerned with preserving its interests to the south, in California, than getting involved in Anglo-American affairs. In the Treaty of Florida (1819), Spain surrendered its claims to the two opposite corners of the United States—the southeast and the northwest. Great Britain had no interest in Florida, but the Oregon country was another matter. The two countries continued to argue over the "Oregon question" for almost thirty years, until a treaty was negotiated in 1846 that finally established the boundary between Canada and the United States. In 1848 the bill to organize Oregon territory was signed by President James K. Polk. In 1853 the area north of the Columbia River was designated Washington Territory.

Even before the formal acquisition of the Oregon/Washington territory—as early as the 1820s and 1830s—mountaineers and guides were leading parties of emigrants, soldiers, missionaries, and fur traders over parts of what would soon come to be called the Oregon Trail. By the 1840s the westward flow had picked up, with about a thousand persons taking part in one enormous expedition—the "Great Migration" of 1843.

The Gold Rush affected this region when the yellow metal was discovered in the Selkirk ranges in Washington in the mid-1850s. The boom, while never rivaling the California frenzy, lasted until the 1880s. The population increase helped stimulate other economic activities in the region, such as cattle raising, lumbering, and agriculture. Fishing and clamming in Puget Sound, Washington (as we will see in the song), became important industries as well.

❋

"Acres of Clams" is typical of a traditional narrative ballad where the singer "has been everywhere and done everything."

> *I was born about ten thousand years ago,*
> *There ain't nothing in the world I do not know.*
> *I saw Peter, Paul and Moses playing ring around the roses,*
> *And I'll whip the guy that says it isn't so.*[26]

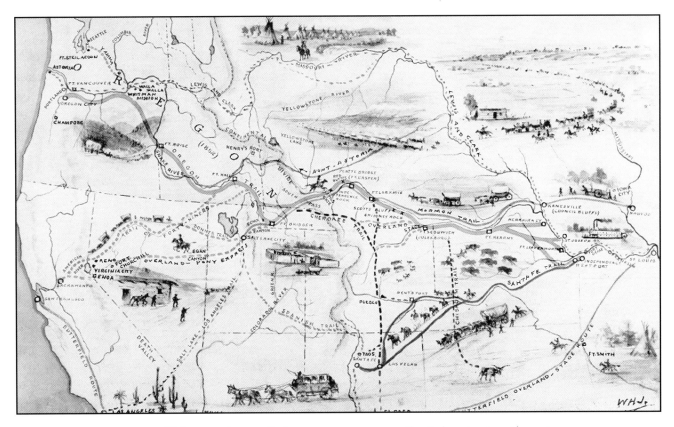

This map shows all the great western trails of the nineteenth century, including the Oregon Trail. More than six thousand settlers traveled west along the Oregon Trail between 1843 and 1846 alone. It took each group about six months to complete the hazardous 2,400-mile (3,800-kilometer) journey.

By the time the singer of this song has gotten to Puget Sound he has tried nearly everything (mining, farming, lumbering) in an attempt to "make it." He symbolizes the entire westward movement of the American settlers. Unfortunately for him, he has been "frequently sold"—that is, cheated and swindled, or, as down-on-their-luck settlers put it, "Busted, disgusted and can't be trusted!"

The tune of "Acres of Clams" was borrowed from a well-known Irish ballad entitled "Old Rosin, the Beau." This was neither the first nor the last time that this wonderful melody had been outfitted with new words. It surfaced as a campaign song for William Henry Harrison in the presidential election campaign of 1840 as "Old Tippecanoe." In 1844, as "Two Dollars a Day and Roast Beef," it helped James K. Polk defeat Henry Clay. In the campaign of 1860, it reappeared as "Lincoln and Liberty." It continued as a good-luck song for the winning side in 1888, when Benjamin Harrison used it to beat Grover Cleveland. But when Harrison tried it once again against Cleveland four years later, it backfired—Cleveland won.

RECOMMENDED LISTENING

Spider John Koerner, *Nobody Knows the Trouble I've Seen*. Red House Records 12.

ACRES OF CLAMS

I've wan - dered all o - ver this coun - try, Pros - pec - ting and

dig - ging for gold. I've tun - neled, hy - drau-licked and cra - dled,

And I have been fre - quent - ly sold.

Chorus

And I have been fre - quent - ly sold, And I have been

The chords above the staves: Bm, A7, D (first system); G, D, A7, D (second system).

Lyrics under the staves:

fre - quent - ly sold. I've tun - neled, hy - drau - licked and

cra - dled, And I have been fre - quent - ly sold.

2) For one who gets riches by mining,
   Perceiving that hundreds grow poor,
   I made up my mind to try farming,
   The only pursuit that is sure. . .

   Chorus: The only pursuit that is sure. . .

3) So, rolling my grub in a blanket,
   I left all my tools on the ground;
   And I started one morning to shank it
   For the country they call Puget Sound.

   Chorus: For the country. . .

4) Arriving flat broke in midwinter,
   The ground was enveloped in fog;
   And covered all over with timber
   Thick as hair on the back of a dog.

   Chorus: Thick as hair. . .

5) When I looked at the prospects so gloomy
   The tears trickled over my face;
   And I thought that my travels had brought me
   To the end of the jumping-off place.

   Chorus: To the end. . .

6) I staked me a claim in the forest
   And set myself down to hard toil.
   For two years I chopped and I struggled,
   But I never got down to the soil.

   Chorus: But I never. . .

7) I tried to get out of the country,
   But poverty forced me to stay.
   Until I became an old settler,
   Then nothing could drive me away.

   Chorus: Then nothing. . .

8) And now that I'm used to the country,
   I think that if man ever found
   A place to live easy and happy,
   That Eden is on Puget Sound.

   Chorus: That Eden. . .

9) No longer the slave of ambition,
   I laugh at the world and its shams;
   As I think of my happy condition,
   Surrounded by acres of clams.

   Chorus: Surrounded by acres. . .

# Notes

1. "An Invitation to North America"—complete words and music in *Immigrant Song Book*.
2. "We Are Traveling to North America"—*ibid*.
3. "America Song"—*ibid*.
4. "When From Italy We Did Take Our Leave"—*ibid*.
5. "Columbus, I Give You the First Prize"—*ibid*.
6. Horace Greeley (1811–1872): founder of *The New York Tribune*; staunch opponent of slavery; defeated by Ulysses S. Grant in the presidential election of 1872.
7. "My Home's Across The Smoky Mountains"—complete words and music in the *Folk Song Encyclopedia, Vol. 2*.
8. "The E-ri-e Canal"—complete words and music in *Songs of the Sea, Rivers, Lakes & Canals*.
9. "America Song"—complete Norwegian and English words and music in *Immigrant Song Book*.
10. "I Have Finished Packing"—*ibid*.
11. "The Mississippi"—complete French and English words and music in *Immigrant Song Book*.
12. "Bread and Roses"—complete words and music in *Folk Song Encyclopedia, Vol. 1*.
13. "Scots Wha Hae"—complete words and music in *Folk Song Encyclopedia, Vol. 2*.
14. "The Death of Crockett"—complete words in *Sound Off*.
15. "The Life of a California Gold Seeker"—complete words and music in *Immigrant Song Book*.
16. "Twelve Hundred More"—*Society of California Pioneers* (excerpt from 1870 broadside).
17. "A Long Time Ago"—complete words and music in *Songs of the Sea, Rivers, Lakes & Canals*.

18. "The Praties"—complete words and music in *Songs of Ireland.*
19. "Villikins and His Dinah"—complete words and music in *British & American Victorian Vocal Varieties.*
20. *Eldorado: California and the Forty-Niners.* Bayard Taylor, 1850.
21. "Get Along, Little Dogies"—complete words and music in *Songs Of The West.*
22. "Uncle Sam's Farm"—complete words and music in *Immigrant Song Book.*
23. "Little Old Sod Shanty"—complete words and music in *Songs of the Western Frontier.*
24. "The Kansas Fool"—complete words and music in *Songs of the Great American West.*
25. "The Oregon Trail"—complete words and music in *Songs of the American People.*
26. "I Was Born About Ten Thousand Years Ago"—compete words and music in *Folk Song Encyclopedia.*

 **Further Reading**

Beebe, Lucius, and Charles Clegg. *Hear the Train Blow: A Pictorial Epic of America in the Railroad Age*. New York: Grosset & Dunlap, 1952.

Botkin, B.A. *A Treasury of American Folklore*. New York: Crown, 1944.

Botkin, B.A., ed. *A Treasury of Western Folklore*. New York: Crown, 1951.

Bull, Inez. *Ole Bull's Activities in the United States Between 1843 and 1880*. Smithtown, N.Y.: Exposition Press, 1982.

Dolph, Edward A. *Sound Off*. New York: Farrar & Rhinehart, 1929, 1942.

Hadfield, Charles. *The Canal Age*. New York: Frederick A. Praeger, 1969.

Kemp, Peter, ed. *Encyclopedia of Ships and Sailing*. New York: Crown, 1980.

Lomax, Alan. *The Folksongs of North America*. New York: Doubleday, 1960.

McCague, James. *Moguls and Iron Men: The Story of the First Transcontinental Railroad*. New York: Harper & Row, 1964.

McKay, Richard C. *South Street: A Maritime History of New York*. New York: G.P. Putnam's Sons, 1934.

McPherson, James M. *Battle Cry of Freedom: The Civil War Era*. New York: Oxford University Press, 1988.

Siber, Irwin. *Songs of the Great American West*. New York: Macmillan Co., 1967.

Silverman, Jerry. *The American History Song Book*. Pacific, Mo.: Mel Bay Publications, 1992.

———. *Ballads and Songs of the Civil War*. Pacific, Mo.: Mel Bay Publications, 1993.

———. *Folk Song Encyclopedia*, Vols. 1 & 2. Milwaukee: Hal Leonard, 1975.

———. *Immigrant Song Book.* Pacific, Mo.: Mel Bay Publications, 1992.

———. *Songs of Ireland.* Pacific, Mo.: Mel Bay Publications, 1991.

———. *Songs of the American People.* Pacific, Mo.: Mel Bay Publications, 1993.

———. *Songs of the Sea, Rivers, Lakes & Canals.* Pacific, Mo.: Mel Bay Publications, 1992.

———. *Songs of the Western Frontier.* Pacific, Mo.: Mel Bay Publications, 1991.

———. *Train Songs.* Pacific, Mo.: Mel Bay Publications, 1991.

Withun, William, L., ed. *Rails Across America.* New York: Smithmark, 1993.

Index

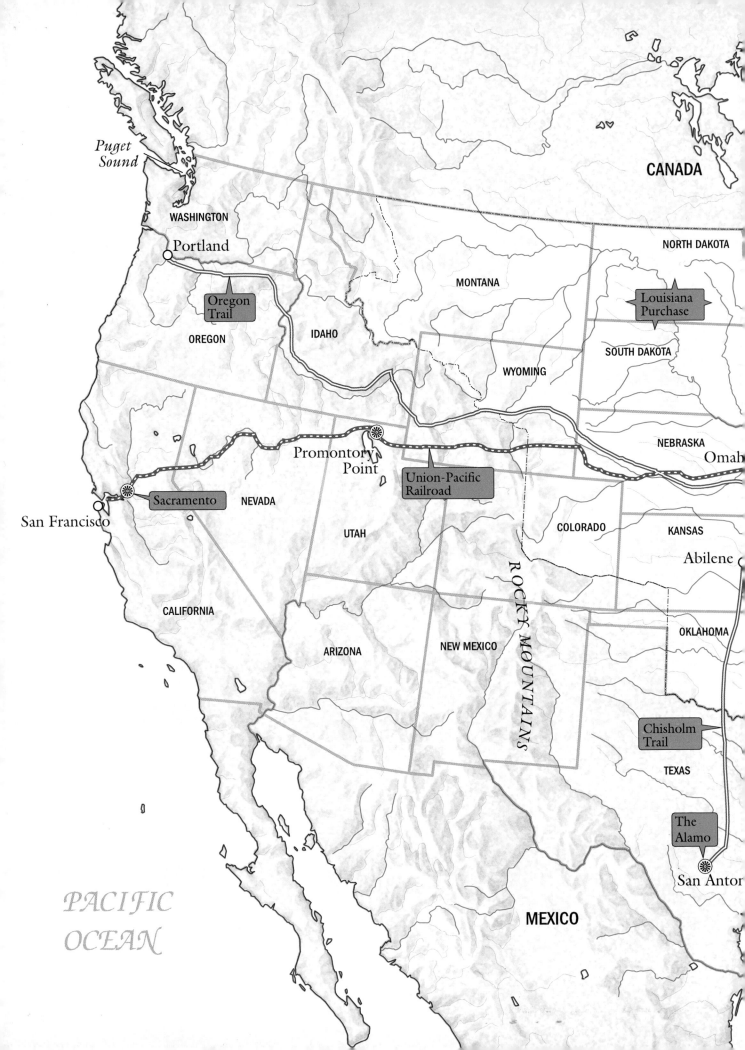